W9-BGN-917

JAMES WATSON

FRANCIS CRICK

Published by Blackbirch Press, Inc.
One Bradley Road
Woodbridge, CT 06525

© 1995 Blackbirch Press, Inc.
First Edition

Printed in Canada

10 9 8 7 6 5 4 3 2 1

Library of Congress Cataloging-in-Publication Data
Sherrow, Victoria.
    Watson and Crick: Decoding the secrets of DNA / by Victoria Sherrow.
        p. cm. — (Partners)
    Includes bibliographical references (p.) and index.
    ISBN 1-56711-133-5 (lib. bdg.)
        1. Watson, James D., 1928—Juvenile literature. 2. Crick, Francis, 1916—Juvenile literature. 3. DNA—Research—Juvenile literature.
4. Molecular biologists—Biography—Juvenile literature. 5. Coopera-tion—Juvenile literature. [1. Watson, James D., 1928- 2. Crick, Francis, 1916- 3. Molecular biologists. 4. DNA—Research.] I. Series.
QP620.S54   1995
574.87'3282—dc20   94-43493
                                                                       CIP
                                                                        AC

JAMES WATSON

FRANCIS CRICK

Decoding the Secrets of DNA

Victoria Sherrow

BLACKBIRCH PRESS

WOODBRIDGE, CONNECTICUT

Table of Contents

James Watson (left) and Francis Crick explain the components of their DNA model.

A Thrilling Discovery

"We weren't the least bit afraid of being

very candid with each other ...

we pooled the way we looked at things ...

we both did it together."

—*Francis Crick*

For thousands of years, people have recognized that offspring resemble their parents—that "like produces like." The seeds of a pea plant sprout into other pea plants; flies give rise only to flies; a pair of mice produces a new generation of mice. The same is true of human beings, who are all born with an assortment of their ancestors' traits. The amazing process by which traits are transmitted from parent to offspring is called heredity. The transmitted unit of heredity, called a gene, is located inside the nucleus (small body near a cell's center containing most of the hereditary material) of living cells.

Until the twentieth century, how genes operated in the process of heredity was a mystery. Although the first living cells were glimpsed under a microscope in the 1600s, further knowledge accumulated gradually. By the 1800s, scientists were studying heredity and had located genes within cells. In 1869, a Swiss scientist found a substance inside the cell nucleus that was later named DNA (short for deoxyribonucleic acid). Scientists proved genes were made of DNA and that DNA was responsible for heredity. But how did it all actually work?

In the 1950s, two young scientists—one British and one American—worked together to unravel the age-old puzzle. By combining their talents and building on the work of others,

Francis Crick and James Watson developed a three-dimensional model for the DNA molecule. In 1953, they announced their discovery, publishing a scientific paper that suggested how DNA functioned in cell reproduction. The news electrified scientists around the world.

This historic discovery came after months of trial-and-error. Inside their London laboratory, the two scientists had spent long hours thinking, reading, studying, and developing various models. Watson contributed his knowledge of biology (especially genetics); while Crick, a physicist, aided in the chemical and physical analysis of the DNA molecule.

When Watson and Crick met in 1951, they quickly found that, despite very different backgrounds and personalities, they were interested in the same scientific questions. Both were eager to solve the mystery of the structure of DNA, a task that Crick later compared to unraveling "a three-dimensional puzzle."[1]

In the years after they solved this "puzzle," Watson and Crick teamed up for other projects, then worked separately as their interests took them in other directions. They received a Nobel Prize and many other honors for their achievements, and enjoy distinguished careers.

The model that the two men constructed—along with their writings on DNA—set off what has been described as a revolution in modern biology. In the years since 1953, hundreds of

Where DNA Is Found

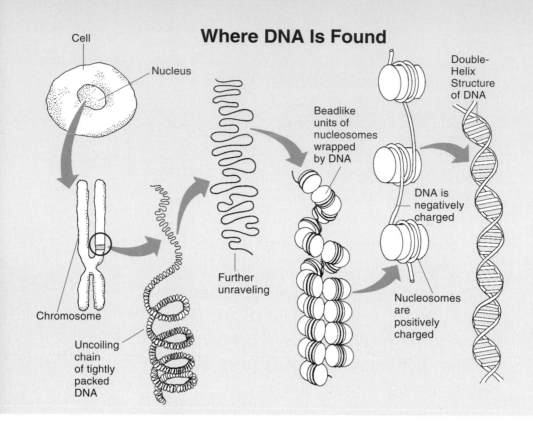

Cell

Nucleus

Chromosome

Uncoiling chain of tightly packed DNA

Further unraveling

Beadlike units of nucleosomes wrapped by DNA

DNA is negatively charged

Nucleosomes are positively charged

Double-Helix Structure of DNA

molecular biologists have chosen to study DNA in the hope of further "cracking the genetic code" and unlocking the ultimate secrets of life, death, health, and disease.

In recent decades, scientists have been able to do things that once would have been labeled science fiction. Genes have been altered and even created. DNA has been transplanted from animals into bacteria, and human genetic material has been placed inside mice eggs, where it produced human protein. DNA technology, including genetic engineering and cloning (a process in which an unfertilized cell's nucleus is replaced with that of another specialized cell), may allow the development of new plants and animals in the lab. Scientists believe that future

DNA research will lead to medical break-throughs.

In addition to these exciting possibilities, there are also potential hazards, such as the creation of new disease-carrying organisms. Because of this, DNA technology is controversial. Knowledge about DNA has affected many areas of life. For example, DNA testing has been used in law enforcement to rule out, or help to convict, suspects. Because of the personalized information it reveals, new scientific knowledge has brought with it numerous ethical dilemmas.

For these reasons, many people cite Watson and Crick's discovery of the structure of DNA as the most significant biological achievement of the century. Asked in 1974 to explain why their scientific partnership had been so successful where many other scientists had tried and failed, Crick said, in part, "We weren't the least bit afraid of being very candid with each other....We pooled the way we looked at things....we both did it together."[2]

Introduction: Notes

1. Francis Crick, *What Mad Pursuit?* (New York: Basic Books, 1988).
2. Franklin H. Portugal and Jack S. Cohen, *A Century of DNA: A History of the Discovery of the Structure and Function of the Genetic Substance* (Cambridge, Mass.: The MIT Press, 1977), 269.

Francis Crick, in his study.

The Urge to Discover

"[He] is a great genius. He really is."

—*Sir Lawrence Bragg, physicist, about*
Francis Crick

Shortly after Francis Harry Compton Crick was born on June 8, 1916, his mother asked her sister to carry him up to the roof of the family's home. This ritual was meant to guarantee that in later life, Francis would "rise to the top." Although Anne Elizabeth Wilkins Crick could not have known it at the time, her first-born child would indeed rise to the top—of the scientific world, as it turned out.

Francis Crick grew up in a comfortable middle-class family near the sprawling town of Northampton in the English Midlands. Francis's father Harry, along with Harry's brother Walter, ran a boot and shoe factory that their father had started. As a child, Francis showed great curiosity. Because his questions went beyond his parents' knowledge, they bought him a children's encyclopedia that contained entries on history, science, mythology, literature, and the arts.

Crick later said he read it avidly. In his autobiography, he wrote:

> It was the science that appealed to me most. What was the universe like? What were atoms? How did things grow? I absorbed great chunks of explanation, reveling in the unexpectedness of it all …How marvelous to have discovered such things! It must have been at such an early age that I decided I would be a scientist.[1]

As a child, Crick worried that by the time he became an adult, all the great scientific discoveries would already have been made. His mother reassured him, "There will be plenty left for you to find out."[2] In the meantime, he conducted various chemistry experiments at home and won a school prize for collecting the most species of wildflowers. He was also a skillful tennis player, as were his father and brother. The family attended church regularly, but during his teens, Crick began to question his own religious beliefs. He began to prefer scientific interpretations for things that traditionally had been explained through religious ideas.

At age fourteen, Crick won a scholarship to Mill Hill School, a private school in northern London (in England, called a public school). The year was 1930, and there was a worldwide economic depression. His family had to work hard so that he could attend this school as a boarding student and take advantage of the excellent science and mathematics programs. After graduating, Crick lived at home while attending University College in London. There, in 1937, he earned his degree in physics, with mathematics as his second area of study.

After graduation, Crick remained at the university to begin working on his doctoral degree, thanks to financial help from his uncle, Arthur Crick. His research professor, Edward Neville da Costa Andrade, later described Crick as "a very able physicist with plenty of initiative."[3] Andrade assigned Crick to study the viscosity of water under pressure at different temperatures. This research was to be the subject for his doctoral thesis, a requirement for the Ph.D. degree.

Crick was close to completing his doctorate when World War II interrupted his plans in 1939. His research laboratory was moved from University College to Wales. In 1940, Crick joined the British Admiralty Research Laboratory, part of the British navy, and married Doreen Dodd. Their son Michael was born in November of that year.

From the Admiralty station in London, Crick was transferred to the Mine Design Department on the southern coast of England. There, he worked to develop radar devices as well as underwater explosives, or noncontact mines, that British aircraft would drop in the Baltic and North seas, to await enemy ships.

During the war, a landmine destroyed the laboratory in Wales that contained the device

Crick and his colleagues had made to measure the viscosity of water at elevated temperatures. Crick later admitted that, at the time, he had already lost interest in that line of research and was relieved to abandon it.

After the war, Crick continued as an Admiralty scientist, working on designs for magnetic and acoustic mines. By then, he was close to thirty years old and found himself doing a lot of soul-searching, evaluating what he had achieved thus far and looking at his future goals. It seemed to him that he had no real expertise in any field. But rather than viewing this as a negative, he saw it as an asset—a chance to take a fresh look at what he actually wanted to do and make a change.

What appealed to him most was fundamental research—making new discoveries—rather than applied research, in which he would use the theories of others in his work. He had been reading *What Is Life?* by Austrian physicist Erwin Schrödinger, published in 1943, that was to inspire many scientists. Crick later remarked that *What Is Life?* impressed him with its imaginative ideas, saying, "It suggested that biological problems could be *thought* about in physical terms—and thus it gave the impression that exciting things in this field were not far off."[4]

Crick was fascinated by Schrödinger's suggestion that new theories in physics could soon explain how molecules were put together in

What appealed to Crick most was fundamental research—making new discoveries.

living cells. Schrödinger said that quantum mechanics (a branch of physics that offers explanations for the physical nature of matter) would contribute a great deal to biology.

As Francis Crick read more about the life sciences, it was cellular biology (or cytology, the study of cells) that intrigued him most. By the late 1940s, it was known that cells are the basic units of life that make up all plants and animals. Cells have been compared to factories where a variety of complex processes are carried out. They contain within themselves the materials and information needed to make proteins and to maintain, repair, and reproduce themselves. Despite their tiny size—cells cannot be viewed with the naked human eye—each contains trillions of atoms in groups called molecules. These molecules play different roles in the functioning of the cell.

It was the molecules inside living cells that Crick now felt drawn to study. At the same time, he wanted to use his knowledge of physics. He struggled to decide what type of research would allow him to best use his skills and fulfill his interests. He narrowed the choice down to either the study of molecules or the higher nervous system (with a focus on the physical nature of consciousness). After turning the matter over in his mind for several weeks, he eventually chose the field that would later be known as molecular biology because he thought his background as a physicist "was more relevant [to that field]."[5]

Crick was also motivated by a personal development. He had become an atheist—a person who does not believe in the existence of God as the supernatural force that created the world. He believed that physics and chemistry could explain much of what organized religions considered the mysteries of their faith, knowable only by God.

Since he had never formally studied biology, Crick set out to learn it on his own by reading piles of books and scientific papers. Reading for hours on end would remain a lifelong habit. His colleague, physicist Lawrence Bragg, would later say of him "[H]e is a great genius. He really is. He reads voraciously."[6]

Among Crick's reading matter at that time were articles by the Nobel-Prize-winning American biochemist Linus Pauling (1901–1994). In 1946, Crick attended one of Pauling's lectures. Pauling had been incorporating theories and approaches from various sciences—chemistry, physics, and biology—into his research. This approach had helped him to understand the mechanics of chemical bonding—the way in which atoms join together to form molecules of various substances. Using quantum mechanics, Pauling had explained the forces that hold atoms together within a molecule. He had shown that atoms join together in definite and predictable patterns. He had also studied how the shapes of various cells in the human body are related to their functions. His landmark 1939 book, *The Nature of the Chemical Bond*, was a valuable information source for many scientists.

Pauling's work shows how the boundaries among the various sciences became blurred during the 1900s as scientists studied living cells. Schrödinger's book, *What Is Life?*, had spurred this trend. Pauling had initially studied chemistry, then physics and biology, in order to answer questions about the structure and function of living cells. Chemistry had taught him much about the structure and properties of atoms and molecules. From the physical sciences, he had gained insight into matter and energy and the interaction between them. The biological sciences explained the nature of living organisms and their life processes. Eventually, the discovery of the structure of DNA would likewise involve a multi-disciplinary research approach.

As he moved into a new area of science, Francis Crick thought carefully about the best place to do his research. He consulted the biophysicist A. V. Hill, who advised him to go work at Strangeways Laboratory in Cambridge, where he could learn more about biology and biophysical techniques (methods of research that blend biology and physics). To promote biophysical research, Great Britain's Medical Research Council (MRC) was awarding grants to physicists entering the field of biology. Crick received one of these.

At the Strangeways Laboratory, a group of scientists were working under Dr. Honor Fell, studying cells. From 1947 to 1949, Crick worked with Dr. Fell (later proclaimed a Dame of the British Empire) to analyze the movement of magnetic particles in cells. But Crick was restless to move onto something he found more interesting.

Around this time, he met Maurice Wilkins, a research scientist at King's College Laboratory in London. Born in New Zealand, Wilkins had lived most of his life in England, where he had earned his doctoral degree in physics. During World War II, Wilkins worked for the British component of the Manhattan Project, which built the world's first atomic bomb.

Like Crick, Wilkins had been impressed by the book *What Is Life?* and had decided to do research that would merge biology and physics. At St. Andrew's University in Scotland, Wilkins studied the effect of ultrasonic waves on genetic material. When the head of that research unit was appointed director of the laboratory at King's College in London, Wilkins went along with him.

At King's College, Maurice Wilkins analyzed living cells with newly developed, powerful x-ray diffraction techniques. Aiming x-rays through slides containing samples of crystallized

The development of powerful new microscopes led to major new discoveries about the nature of cells.

☙☙☙☙☙☙

molecules, they then directed those rays onto photographic film. The resulting technique was called x-ray crystallography.

Soon, Wilkins was concentrating on nucleic acids, those molecules usually found inside the nuclei of cells. By 1948, he was convinced x-ray crystallography would enable him to learn more about the structure of these substances. Stronger microscopes had led to important findings about nucleic acids during the 1920s and 1930s. Scientists knew that there were two kinds of nucleic acid—RNA (ribonucleic acid) and DNA (deoxyribonucleic acid).

The chemical make-up of these two kinds of nucleic acid was similar, which led to confusion during the years when they were first identified. During the 1800s, scientists had speculated that RNA was found only in plants, while DNA was confined to the cells of animals. Then, in 1922, scientists found RNA in an animal's pancreatic cell. Others found DNA in some plant cells.

By 1938, it was clear that both RNA and DNA were found in all cells, whether plant or animal. Later discoveries determined that they were also present in viruses and that some were located in parts of the cell that were outside the nucleus. By the late 1940s, scientists thought that nucleic acids must play a role in heredity, but exactly which role remained unknown. Maurice Wilkins and Francis Crick were soon to play major roles in answering those questions.

In 1949, at age thirty-three, Crick was older than most people at work on a doctoral degree. Still, he began a new line of research: x-ray diffraction studies of protein molecules.

During this time, changes had taken place in Crick's personal life as well. His first marriage had ended. During the war, he had met Odile Speed, then an officer in the British women's naval service, and they were married in 1949.

Crick was pleased when he heard that Max Perutz, an Austrian-born physicist known for his research on blood molecules, had been named director of a new MRC Unit of Molecular Biology. It would be located at the Cavendish Laboratory in Cambridge, near London. The unit would use x-ray diffraction techniques to study protein molecules. Proteins are integral chemical components of cells, serving as enzymes (chemical tools) or molecular building blocks. To Crick, it seemed an ideal setting in which to learn more about the structure of protein molecules. He was delighted when Perutz approved his application to join the Cavendish group.

Considering Crick's limited income as a research scientist, he and Odile were happy to find an inexpensive apartment within walking distance of the laboratory. It had been occupied by the Perutzes, who left to move to a large home in the suburbs.

Perutz was impressed by Crick's intelligence and later said that he showed "a lively interest, a remarkably clear and analytical mind and a capacity for quickly grasping the essence of any problem."[7] Crick began his research with the goal of writing a doctoral thesis called "Polypeptides and Proteins." Crick finally completed the thesis and received his doctorate in 1953, after he and Watson unveiled their DNA structure.

Shortly after he arrived at "the Cavendish," as the lab was known, Crick also conducted a critical review of the work that had already been done by Max Perutz and John Kendrew. Crick disagreed with their approach and conclusion that the hemoglobin molecule (the oxygen-carrying molecule in red blood cells) had a regular geometric structure. Later research by Sir Lawrence Bragg would show that globular proteins (the group that included hemoglobin) do not have regular geometric structures.

Perutz and Kendrew accepted Crick's criticism, but some other scientists regarded him as a brash, presumptuous newcomer. Dr. Lawrence Bragg was among those who told Crick he was out of line, at one point, saying, "Crick, you're rocking the boat."[8] Crick later wrote that Bragg "came to regard me as a nuisance who…talked too much and in too critical a manner."[9] Later, they grew to like and respect each other. Crick especially appreciated Bragg's enthusiasm for science and his unpretentiousness.

As he continued to study protein molecules at the Cavendish, Crick became proficient in the techniques of x-ray crystallography. He learned how to mount crystals on a slide and take x-rays of them, which resulted in pictures that showed a great deal about the physical dimensions of the cells being studied. Such pictures could also reveal clues to the molecular structure of cells.

Francis Crick was busily engaged in his work in 1951 when James Watson, a young American scientist, arrived at the Cavendish. Crick soon realized that they shared a strong common interest. In less than two years, that interest was to lead to one of the most significant scientific discoveries of all time.

Chapter 1: Notes

1. Crick, 8–9.
2. Crick, 9.
3. Quoted in L. Olby, "Francis Crick, DNA and the Central Dogma," *Daedalus*, vol. 99 (1970); 941.
4. Quoted in Horace Freeland Judson, *The Eighth Day of Creation: The Makers of the Revolution in Biology* (New York: Simon and Schuster, 1979), 109.
5. Ibid.
6. Ibid.
7. Quoted in Portugal and Cohen, 228.
8. Crick, 50.
9. Ibid.

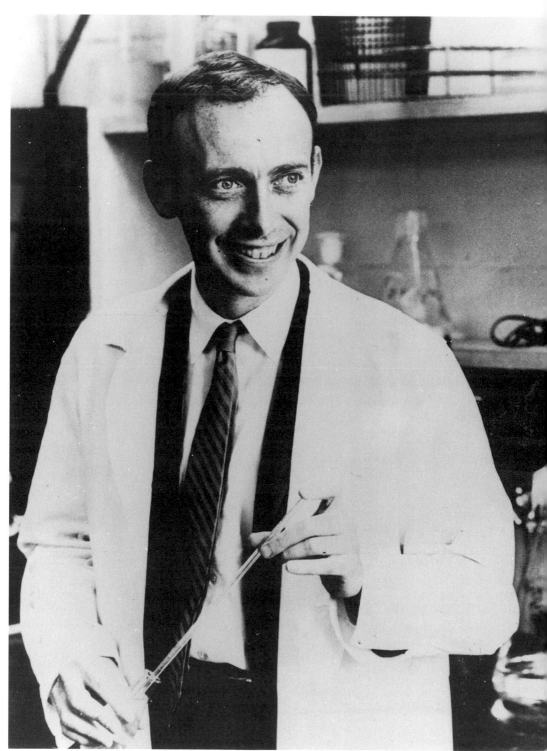

James Watson, at the Cavendish laboratory.

From Quiz-Kid
to Biologist

"From my first day in the lab,

I knew I would not leave Cambridge

for a long time."

—*James Watson*

Francis Crick was twelve years old when his future scientific partner, James Dewey Watson, was born an ocean away, in Chicago, Illinois. The Watsons welcomed their second child and first son on April 6, 1928. Clever and curious from his earliest days, James Watson seemed destined for a bright future. A slightly built, somewhat shy child, he spent much of his time alone or playing with his sister Elizabeth, nicknamed Betty.

While Watson was growing up, America was struggling through the worst economic period in its history, the Great Depression, which began in 1929. During this time, millions of people lost their jobs and homes, and families were hard-pressed to buy even the basic necessities.

To help make ends meet, Mrs. Watson worked in the admissions department of the University of Chicago, later moving to its housing department. With their limited means, the Watson family could not afford to give their children luxuries like private schooling. However, the family valued education and the arts and encouraged James and Elizabeth to also appreciate them. One of James's uncles was a lecturer at the Art Institute of Chicago.

At school, James impressed people with his quick intelligence and remarkable memory. Chicago was then the site of a popular radio show called "Quiz Kids." No one was surprised when the producer, Louis Cowan, chose James Watson as one of the young people to appear regularly on the program. As a contestant, he competed with top students from all over the country, answering questions about history, science, literature, and other subjects.

As Watson was entering his teens, the Great Depression was ending and World War II was beginning. During those years, he was particularly interested in animals, especially birds. He belonged to a bird-watching organization and spent hours studying these creatures.

Watson was still concentrating on zoology when he entered the University of Chicago in 1943 after completing high school at the early age of fifteen. The university was known for its strong science program; some of the world's most prominent scientists had taught and conducted research there. Among them was America's first Nobel Prize winner in physics, Albert A. Michelson, who had calculated the velocity of light, laying the groundwork for Einstein's theory of relativity. Another Nobel laureate and faculty member, Enrico Fermi, had led a brilliant team of physicists who were studying atomic power. Under his direction, they developed the world's first self-sustaining nuclear chain reaction. Their special lab was built and operated in secret under the squash courts at the university in 1942.

In college, James Watson "never took any notes and yet at the end of the course he came [in at the] top of the class."

❦❦❦❦❦❦

It was into this stimulating atmosphere that James Watson stepped when he entered college. Living at home to save money, he rode a streetcar to and from classes. As a freshman, he began a carefully planned curriculum designed to give students a basic, all-around education in mathematics, literature, philosophy, and science. A zoology major, Watson focused on ornithology (the study of birds). As he had in high school, he amazed his teachers with his remarkable memory. One of his professors, Paul Weiss, later wrote that Watson "never took any notes and yet at the end of the course he came [in at the] top of the class."[1]

Despite his excellent grades, Watson shied away from taking advanced physics or chemistry courses. He later explained, "I was principally interested in birds and managed to avoid taking any chemistry or physics courses which looked of even medium difficulty."[2]

Out of personal interest, he did sit in on a course in population genetics taught by a well-known mathematician named Sewall Wright. At the time, Watson still planned eventually to become a bird curator at a prominent museum, such as the Field Museum in Chicago or the American Museum of Natural History in New York City. Toward that goal, he spent the summer after he finished college studying botany (the science of plants) and ornithology at the University of Michigan.

After finishing his three-year program, Watson took an additional year of zoology courses and received his bachelor's degree in 1947. Yet, his brief exposure to genetics during college had captured his interest. It seemed to him that genetics—the study of heredity, or how traits are passed on from one generation to the next—might be the most exciting field confronting the scientists of his day.

Around that time, he read *What Is Life?*, by Erwin Schrödinger—just as Francis Crick had— and became even more drawn to the field of genetics. Watson was absolutely fascinated by Schrödinger's theories about the possible atomic and molecular roots of life. Schrödinger's use of the principles of quantum mechanics to examine the nature of the gene made a great deal of sense to Watson. He could see that quantum mechanics, which deals with the behavior of atoms and subatomic particles (the nucleus, protons, and electrons), must surely have important applications in physics, chemistry, and biology.

On his own, Watson continued to read about genetics. But he feared that, since he had not taken advanced college chemistry, he would not be able to enroll in any high-level genetics courses. Later, he said, "It was my hope that the gene might be solved without my learning any chemistry."[3]

When he applied to graduate schools, Watson was turned down by both Harvard University and the California Institute of Technology (Caltech). He and his father visited Indiana University, a school that had offered him a research fellowship to pursue his doctoral degree. His initial application to the university had stated that he planned to study ornithology. The head of the graduate department told him that he should go elsewhere if that was still his plan. Watson explained that he was now interested in genetic research.

One of the attractions at Indiana University was the presence of geneticist Hermann Muller (1890–1967). Professor Muller had worked with an American geneticist and Nobel laureate, Thomas Hunt Morgan (1866–1945), at Columbia University in New York City, where they did pioneering research on heredity.

When Morgan began his work in the late 1800s, scientists were puzzling over how living things grow from cells to fully formed organisms and how traits are passed from parent to offspring. Before Morgan, an Austrian monk named Gregor Mendel (1822–1884) had conducted landmark studies on heredity. In 1865, Mendel wrote a paper describing his numerous experiments with pea plants. For years, he had grown the plants while recording the traits of each generation. Mendel wondered if there were set patterns, or laws, of inheritance. Why, he puzzled, did some traits disappear in one generation only to reappear in later generations?

Why did some traits pass on, unchanged, to new generations while other traits were a blend of characteristics from both parents?

His research led Mendel to conclude that organisms receive two factors, one from each parent, for a given trait, such as the green or yellow color of peas. He stated that some traits are dominant (controlling) and others are recessive. He then theorized that if an organism inherits both types of factors, the dominant factor masks the expression of the recessive trait. Yet, recessive traits are passed along, too, and may reappear in later generations if an organism receives a recessive factor from both parents. Mendel also found that he could predict the ratio of different traits that would occur in new generations of plants.

Gregor
Mendel

A Dutch biologist, Hugo De Vries, carried Mendel's theories further. Studying flowers, De Vries noted that some had shapes that differed from the norm. He called these changes mutations (from the Latin word *mutare*—"to change"). Because he saw that mutations could occur in one or just some parts of a plant, De Vries concluded that the traits themselves must be located, and passed on, in separate units. These "units" of inheritance would later be called genes.

The location of these hereditary units was still unclear at that time. Some scientists however, thought that they were contained in chromosomes—the long, coiled, threadlike structures found in living cells and viruses.

In 1902, Walter Stanborough Sutton announced that he believed chromosomes come in pairs, with each of the two segments having a similar structure. In human cells, said Sutton, the 46 chromosomes should be viewed as 23 pairs. A new human being is formed by the union of a sperm cell and an egg cell, each of which contains just 23 chromosomes. When they merge, said Sutton, the newly formed cell receives the correct number: 46 chromosomes, or 23 pairs.

A few years later, two British scientists, William Bateson and R. C. Punnett, tested some of De Vries's and Sutton's theories with their own experiments. They concluded that factors for individual traits might not always be independent, as De Vries had thought, but instead are sometimes combined. In that way, certain traits are always passed on together.

Other facets of genetics were explored earlier by Charles Darwin, a British scientist. In 1831, Darwin embarked on a worldwide ocean voyage. Observing the amazing variety of plants and animals around him, Darwin filled notebooks with his observations. He wondered why the fossils of some animals that had become extinct resembled certain living animals. He marveled that animals often had traits that were exactly suited to life in their surroundings—the color and shape of green insects living on plant leaves, for instance. On the Galapagos Islands, he saw that different kinds of finches had different beaks, which enabled them to eat different foods, thus avoiding competition.

In his 1859 book, *The Origin of the Species*, Darwin proposed that all life on earth had evolved gradually through the ages from very simple, single cells to highly complex, multi-celled organisms. His theory of evolution through natural selection suggested that, in nature, those organisms with advantages over others had the best chance to survive and repro-duce. Injurious traits, said Darwin, "would be rigidly destroyed."[4]

Thomas Hunt Morgan doubted some of Mendel's and Darwin's conclusions and hoped to discover how inherited traits could undergo changes through the years as organisms faced changing conditions. He set up experiments to learn about mutations and to see whether some traits were "linked" with others. For these tests, he bred millions of *Drosophila melanogaster*, commonly called "fruit flies." Only two days after mating, female flies lay hundreds of eggs. Within 10 to 15 days, those eggs hatch and become adults. Because they have just four pairs of chromosomes, these insects are easier to study than more complex organisms.

Hoping to cause mutations, Morgan exposed the flies to extreme heat and cold, large amounts

Charles Darwin proposed that all life on earth had evolved gradually through the ages from simple, single cells to highly complex organisms.

of salt and sugar, and other unnatural conditions. One day in 1909 he found a white-eyed
fly among the scores of red-eyed ones—he had
precipitated a mutation! By mating this fly and
studying later generations, he realized that
Mendel had been correct in some of his findings
regarding the ratio of traits.

The same year that Morgan found the white-
eyed fly in his lab, a Danish botanist, Wilhelm
Johannsen, gave a name to the units on chromosomes thought to contain hereditary traits. He
called them genes, from a Greek word that
means "to give birth to." But no one had yet
seen a gene, nor would they until high-powered
microscopes were invented in the 1940s. Without visible proof of genes, scientists continued to
argue about the existence of the gene during the
early 1900s.

For his part, Morgan decided that genes did
exist and that they were located in rows along
chromosomes. He was more sure of this when
he discovered that longer chromosomes seemed
to hold more traits. Morgan also showed that
certain traits were linked. In the flies, for example, the trait of white eyes was connected to
maleness, with both traits being located on the
same chromosome, thus providing a physical
explanation for Mendel's observations. Linkage
helped to explain how pairs of chromosomes
could pass on so many, different traits. Morgan
suggested that when genes for more than one

trait stay linked on the same chromosome, they will be passed on together. He announced the theory of linkage in July 1910.

More discoveries followed. Morgan became the first scientist to identify which chromosomes contained which traits in fruit flies. By 1912, he and his associates, Calvin Bridges, Hermann J. Muller, and Alfred H. Sturtevant had studied forty different mutations, including crooked bodies and abnormally small wings. They also published a landmark book, *The Mechanism of Mendelian Heredity,* in 1915, as well as "gene maps" that showed where traits could be found along the chromosomes of fruit flies.

Morgan also devised a theory of how linked traits could become "unlinked." This event seemed to occur during cell division, when chromosomes became wrapped around each other or overlapped. During this "crossing over," as Morgan called it, chromosomes could break, and the broken pieces could join together in different, new ways. A Danish biologist, F. A. Janssen, had noticed this in 1909.

When James Watson arrived at Indiana University, Hermann Muller had just won a Nobel Prize for his discovery, in the 1920s, that x-rays can cause mutations in genes. Muller had planned specific mutations, then produced them by using x-rays on fruit fly chromosomes. In effect, he had developed new forms of life inside the laboratory, generating flies with new and

Muller had, in effect, developed new forms of life inside the laboratory.

different types of eyes, bodies, wings, and coloration, along with new combinations of these traits. In 1921, he had accurately predicted that the study of bacterial viruses would result in genetic breakthroughs.

At Indiana, Watson finally did study advanced organic chemistry (the chemistry of living things) to augment the basic inorganic and organic chemistry he had taken as an undergraduate. Tall and thin, he dressed casually, often wearing tennis shoes to class. According to author Richard Olby, Watson "did not have a fund of small talk" and concentrated on people he regarded as his intellectual equals.[5] Says Olby, "Not all [of his fellow students] liked the way Watson would turn discussions in a direction which was of interest to him, and none liked his habit of opening a book to read when the speaker proved dull or unintelligent."[6]

Watson's graduate supervisor, Salvador Luria, inspired him to study bacteria and viruses. Luria was a brilliant researcher and teacher, known for his work with bacterial viruses (viruses that attack bacteria), the simplest forms of all viruses. Bacterial viruses are called *bacteriophages,* often shortened to "phages."

As Hermann Muller had once predicted, some scientists around the world had begun studying these minute organisms. Luria was learning how phages multiplied, among other things. His colleagues in the United States

included the German-American Max Delbrück,
a quantum physicist turned biologist. One of
Delbrück's early research papers on genetics,
written in 1935, had actually inspired part of
Schrödinger's book, *What Is Life?*

The people studying phages thought their
research would yield important information
about DNA. Some believed that viruses were
made up solely of DNA (although it later turned
out that they consist of about half RNA or DNA
and half protein). That being the case, it made
sense to study the simplest viruses, phages, in
order to learn more about DNA and genetics.

Luria, Delbrück, and others referred to themselves as the "American phage group," and
Watson soon became part of it. In a 1947 paper
called "Growing Up in the Phage Group," he
described this time of his life as happy and exciting.[7] He also took courses in proteins, nucleic
acids, and scientific German. These studies later
proved useful in the DNA research he would
conduct at Cambridge with Francis Crick, who
was likewise studying proteins and nucleic acids
during those years.

During the summer of 1948, Watson went to
Cold Spring Harbor Laboratory in New York
State to attend its annual conference and take
courses in biology and genetics. Scientists from
all over the world regularly attended these semi-
nars, some bringing laboratory equipment in
order to conduct research during their stays. The

scientists could also discuss their work as they enjoyed swims, canoe rides, tennis, baseball games, and other recreational activities. Watson later wrote, "As the summer passed on I liked Cold Spring Harbor more and more, both for its intrinsic beauty and for the honest ways in which good and bad science got sorted out."[8]

After two more years at Indiana University, Watson had completed his doctoral thesis, discussing the lethal effects of x-rays on bacterial viruses. It was accepted, and he received his Ph.D., becoming Dr. James Watson in 1950 at age twenty-two. He planned to remain with the phage group, contributing to new knowledge in the field of bacterial viruses and genetics.

Salvador Luria thought Watson could make a stronger contribution to phage research by learning more about chemistry, especially the chemistry of nucleic acids. Figuring out the chemical structure of the nucleic acid DNA, which makes up genes, might show how genes controlled heredity, said Luria.

While teaching a course in bacterial viruses, another member of the phage group, Max Delbrück, had met a prominent Danish biochemist named Herman Kalckar. Kalckar was studying nucleic acids, and it was agreed that Watson would spend the next year working in his lab in Copenhagen. To fund these postgraduate studies, Watson received a grant from the National Research Council.

In Denmark, Watson bicycled to and from the lab each day. Soon, he found himself spending most of his research time with one of Kalckar's associates, Ole Maaloe, who had lived in America while doing research at the California Institute of Technology. Watson felt he could communicate better with Maaloe than he could with Kalckar. Besides, he still found that he enjoyed phage research more than biochemistry. In his autobiography, Watson wrote,

Within three months Ole and I had finished a set of experiments on the fate of a bacterial-virus particle when it multiplies inside a bacterium to form several hundred new virus particles....On the other hand, it was equally obvious that I had not done anything which was going to tell us what a gene was or how it reproduced. And unless I became a chemist, I could not see how I would. [9]

Watson was pleased when Kalckar suggested that they spend April and May attending a scientific meeting at the Zoological Station in Naples, Italy. There, Watson looked forward to reading about genetics on his own and possibly studying the embryos of marine animals. While in Naples, he began feeling restless as he walked the streets or read journal articles about early genetic studies and research. "Sometimes I daydreamed about discovering the secret of the gene, but not once did I have the faintest trace of a respectable idea," he later wrote. "It was thus difficult to avoid the disquieting thought that I was not accomplishing anything."[10]

"Sometimes I daydreamed about discovering the secret of a gene, but not once did I have the faintest trace of a respectable idea."

These feelings of aimlessness were replaced with excitement when Watson attended a lecture given by Maurice Wilkins. During his presentation, Wilkins showed his audience a few x-ray diffraction photographs of DNA that had been taken in the laboratory at King's College. He explained that by examining these patterns, he and his associates hoped to see details of the molecular structure that had never been visible before. Eventually, this could enable them to identify the types and positions of the atoms in the DNA molecule.

Watson was aware that a number of other scientists, including Linus Pauling, had used x-ray crystallography to learn more about the atomic structure of molecules. Pauling also made a presentation at the Naples meeting, showing models he had made of certain protein molecules. Watson was very impressed by Pauling's research and his use of models to understand chemical structure, a technique he would later suggest to Francis Crick.

As he examined the photographs of DNA, Watson was alert to many new possibilities. He had often worried that the structure of genes might be very complicated and irregular. But now he concluded that if genes could crystallize, they must have a regular structure—"one that could be solved in a straightforward fashion."[11] He later said, "I became polarized toward finding out the secret of the gene."[12]

James Watson demonstrates some of the fine points of the double-helix structure.

Watson was eager to speak with Maurice Wilkins about his findings but could not locate him until the next day when a group of scientists met to tour some Greek ruins. He was disappointed when Wilkins expressed no interest in having Watson join the group at King's College.

James Watson was convinced that he must "learn more about the structure of the molecules which the geneticists talked about so passionately."[13] Looking for a good place to engage in genetic research, he discovered that Max Perutz and John Kendrew were studying large molecules at the Cavendish Laboratory. He wrote a letter to his graduate school advisor, Salvador Luria, asking for advice. Luria wrote back, saying that he had met Kendrew and found out he could use an assistant. Kendrew agreed that James Watson could come to the Cavendish.

There was still another barrier to overcome. Watson had just renewed his fellowship to spend another year at the lab in Denmark. He notified the Fellowship Board of the National Research Council that he wished to change plans and that he had become convinced "that x-ray crystallography was the key to genetics."[14] But he had no guarantee that the board would agree to extend his grant.

Nevertheless, in October 1951, Watson arrived in England with high expectations and great enthusiasm. Dr. Kendrew and his wife offered to rent him a small bedroom in their home, located a short distance from the Cavendish lab. He would later write of that time, "From my first day in the lab, I knew I would not leave Cambridge for a long time…. for I had immediately discovered the fun of talking to Francis Crick."[15]

Chapter 2: Notes

1. Quoted in Richard Olby, *The Path to the Double Helix* (Seattle: University of Washington Press, 1974), 297.
2. James D. Watson, *The Double Helix* (New York: Atheneum, 1968), 21.
3. Watson, 21.
4. Charles Darwin, *The Origin of Species* (New York Random House, 1993), 108.
5. Richard Olby, 298.
6. Ibid.
7. Judson, 65.
8. Quoted in Judson, 67.
9. Watson, 28–29.
10. Watson, 30–31.
11. Watson, 33.
12. Quoted in Judson, 47.
13. Watson, 48.
14. Watson, 43.
15. Watson, 48.

Crick and Watson chat during a break at the Cavendish lab.

A Meeting of Minds

"It was a remarkable thing to find somebody...

who reinforced my own

sense of what was important."

—*Francis Crick*

In later years, neither Francis Crick nor James Watson could recall the exact details of their very first meeting, which occurred at the Cavendish laboratory sometime during the first week of October 1951. Crick told an interviewer years later, "I came home one day…and my wife said to me, 'Oh, Max was round here with a young American, and do you know *he had no hair!*' (What she meant was, he had a crew cut.) And then we must have met, and I don't recall exactly the moment…I remember the chats we had over those first two or three days…."[1]

Crick also remembered being "electrified" by those first encounters. He once fondly recalled, "We both had the same point of view, but he knew all about phage, which I had only read about in books…and I knew all about x-ray diffraction, which he only knew about second-hand. But it was a remarkable thing to find somebody…who reinforced my own sense of what was important."[2]

Working together in the small labs, Watson and Crick shared ideas, information, and their skills. In his autobiography, Watson said they talked for several hours a day: "Often when he was stumped by his equations he used to pump my reservoir of phage lore. At other moments Francis would endeavor to fill my brain with crystallographic facts, ordinarily available only through the painful reading of professional journals."[3] Watson also liked to meet interesting scientists at the Cricks' afternoon teas.

Max Perutz, who observed their developing partnership, later said, "Watson arrived knowing nothing of our work…we—except maybe Crick, who had read more widely—we knew nothing of *his* work. His arrival at that time was extraordinarily opportune."[4] Lawrence Bragg also thought that the two men complemented each other well.

The two scientists began lunching together at a small pub near the lab, often on traditional English dishes—shepherd's pie, sausage and beans, gooseberry pie. Much of their talk centered on DNA. Soon, they were together so often that the directors of the lab gave their unit another room, to be shared specifically by Crick and Watson.

Crick believes that their rapport grew "partly because our interests were astonishingly similar and partly, I suspect, because a certain youthful arrogance, a ruthlessness, and an impatience with sloppy thinking came naturally to both of us. Jim was distinctly more outspoken than I was, but our thought processes were remarkably similar."[5]

As they shared their desire to study and solve the structure of DNA, it became the focus of their research. Watson suggested that they try making models, a practical approach Linus Pauling had used to work out the structure of proteins. They discussed Schrödinger's book, *What Is Life?*, but did not think its theoretical framework would help them to unravel the DNA mystery. Crick later said, "It seemed quite obvious to us that we should follow Pauling."[6]

As they worked on DNA, Watson and Crick reviewed what was known about it up to that time. Scientists had discovered which chemical elements made up the DNA molecule, along with their proportions. The researchers at King's College, among others, had theorized about the physical arrangements these atoms might take in the molecule, but nothing was known for certain.

Pieces of knowledge had accumulated for more than one hundred years. The official discovery of DNA occurred in 1869 when a Swiss chemist, Johann Friedrich Miescher, isolated a powdery gray substance from human white blood cells. He called it "nuclein," since it came from a cell nucleus. The large molecules Miescher had found showed a repetition of slightly different chemical bits. He was not sure what he had encountered, but in time, he realized something quite significant: This material seemed to occur in all cells.

In later studies, Miescher and several other scientists, including a prominent organic American chemist, Pheobus A. Levene, identified three major chemical components of "nuclein": a sugar molecule (ribose or deoxyribose), a phosphate (containing hydrogen, oxygen, and phosphorus), and a nitrogen-containing base that could bond with hydrogen. The presence of phosphate explained why chemical tests of nuclein—or DNA—showed a high phosphorus content.

Later, the DNA molecule was found to be an acid and was renamed nucleic acid. Gradually, the four base chemicals of the molecule were identified. One, named guanine, was found in 1844, in the excreta of birds. It was not until 1884, though, that guanine was isolated as part of the DNA molecule. Another molecular base, adenine, was found in the DNA of cattle pancreas in 1885. Thymine was found in 1893, and then cytosine in 1894. Uracil (the base that is found instead of thymine in RNA) was isolated in 1900. Since this occurred before 1922, scientists still mistakenly thought that RNA was found just in plants while DNA occurred only in animals.

Now scientists were left wondering about the total number of nucleotides that made up DNA, as well as the way these nucleotides were arranged. Later, scientists saw that DNA was a large molecule (macromolecule) in the shape of a long, threadlike chain.

During the 1930s, two American scientists, George W. Beadle and Edward L. Tatum, found that DNA plays a key role in the growth process. Beadle had theorized that DNA controls the production of enzymes—protein substances that regulate the speed of chemical reactions in the body while remaining unchanged themselves. He and Tatum exposed molds to radiation and found that the molds' offspring could no longer produce the foodstuff that healthy molds normally make on their own. The molds' genes had mutated and lost the ability to manufacture the enzymes that molds needed to live.

During the late 1940s, an Austrian-American biochemist, Erwin Chargaff, made important new findings. Studying cells from numerous organisms, Chargaff found DNA in all of them. He measured the chemical bases—adenine *(A)*, guanine *(G)*, thymine *(T)*, and cytosine *(C)*—and calculated the relative amounts of each. He found that DNA molecules included the same amounts of guanine and cytosine. The amounts of adenine and thymine were also equivalent. This held true no matter from which animal his DNA sample had come—fish, mammal, or insect.

Scientist Sven Furberg, a Swede working in London during the late 1940s, proposed some structural models for DNA. Furberg's ideas did not fit all that was then known about the density of the DNA molecule, but they corrected some misconceptions. He placed the sugar molecules at right angles to the bases (*A, G, T,* and *C*), whereas others had wrongly put them in parallel positions. Later, Watson and Crick said that Furberg had made an essential contribution to their ultimate findings.

In 1951, British scientist Alexander Todd and his colleagues supplied another missing piece of DNA chemistry. Todd found that in the backbone of the molecule, the third carbon in the sugar ring was linked to the phosphate, which, in turn, was linked to the fifth carbon of the next sugar, and so on, in a repeating pattern.

As they worked on the structure of DNA, Watson and Crick mulled over these findings and sought to apply them. Looking at Linus Pauling's discovery of the alpha helix form for proteins, they wondered if DNA might be some type of helix, or spiraling shape. During these days, Watson expressed a worry—what if the structure of DNA turned out to be "very dull," giving few clues to how DNA replicated itself and controlled cell chemistry?[7]

By this time, scientists knew that hereditary traits were located, and often linked, on genes, which were located on chromosomes inside the cell nucleus. But how could such minute molecular units hold so many, various traits? And how did DNA reproduce itself, causing "like to produce like" in millions of different plants and animals? Scientists hoped that the structure of DNA would answer those questions.

Watson worried that the actual structure of DNA would turn out to be "very dull."

Crick believed that in order for Darwin's theory of natural selection to work, something in an organism must carry genetic information, or instructions. That information must do something useful or produce other things that do necessary jobs in a cell so that the organism can survive and reproduce. There must then be a process for exact replication of this information—in effect, a copying mechanism. Such replication must, in turn, produce entities that can likewise be copied. These replications had probably been going on for millions of years—an amazing feat.

As he considered the work done with cell enzymes, Crick wondered exactly *how* they were made and how DNA was involved. Each gene (or mutant of a gene) seemed to control one enzyme, so Crick was among those who first concluded that each gene on a chromosome governs a particular protein. These proteins would be building blocks for cells or would act as catalysts, deciding which chemical reactions should and should not take place in the cell.[8]

Although Watson and Crick knew much about the chemical make-up of DNA, the basic problem of its structure remained unsolved. How did those chemical bits fit into a three-dimensional frame that allowed DNA to continually produce copies of itself?

Hoping for clues to the DNA structure, they continued to scrutinize the latest photographs

obtained by x-ray crystallography. The same
year that Watson arrived at Cambridge, Dr.
Rosalind Franklin, an outstanding crystallographer, came to King's College Laboratory. Born
in England, Franklin had been educated as a
physical chemist at Cambridge, then had worked
in Paris from 1947 to 1951. At King's College,
she applied her expertise to biological studies,
focusing on research with DNA fibers. Her
photos proved extremely valuable to Watson and
Crick in their DNA research. In fact, Franklin
herself came close to discovering the structure of
DNA first. Scientific historians would later say
that she did not do so only because she worked
in isolation and approached the problem quite
systematically, verifying details slowly, each step
of the way.

Pictures taken at King's College showed
DNA molecules from a variety of living things
had similar outlines on photographs. Maurice
Wilkins noted that the molecular fibers had a
uniform arrangement. He had also found that
moister fibers made better slides for x-ray
crystallograpy purposes than the dried fibers that
had been used most often in the past. As he
analyzed his photos, Wilkins was stricken with
the basic simplicity of the molecule.

Like Crick, Watson had become friends with
Maurice Wilkins, and they had regular conversa-
tions. The three scientists—Watson, Crick, and
Wilkins—agreed that the DNA molecule might

well take the form of a helix, often compared to a spiraling staircase. The molecule seemed to be the same width all along its length, and it appeared to be a dense molecule.

As with the chemical studies, nothing in the photographs explained how so many very different traits were transmitted by a molecule that had a similar shape and chemical composition, regardless of the organism involved. Watson and Crick suggested that the group at King's College try making three-dimensional models, but no one there seemed interested in doing so.

Other scientists, including Linus Pauling, were also interested in DNA and in the x-ray pictures from King's College. Pauling, too, seriously considered the idea that the molecule was a helix. But even if that were true, there were still many details to work out: For example, how many strands (chains) of atoms did the helix contain? If two or three, then was the backbone of the chains on the inside or the outside of the helix, if it even was a helix? How were the nucleotides spaced?

Working together on these problems, Watson and Crick found that their styles of research complemented one another. Crick tended to look at things in a concrete, more structural way. Watson, on the other hand, had a more functional and abstract style. Both were receptive to unfamiliar ideas and approaches. As they worked together exchanging thoughts, new ideas and solutions seemed to emerge.

In the fall of 1951, they ordered custom-made metal parts from a factory for use in making three-dimensional models. They needed metal pieces to represent the DNA bases, the five-sided sugar molecules, and the phosphates—as well as wires and other materials. During the months to come, these pieces would be arranged in various versions of DNA. At first, they did not seem to fit together in any logical way.

Others working with DNA were likewise baffled. They wondered where to place the backbones—the frame of the molecule that would hold the bases. Like some, Linus Pauling was considering a three-strand model of DNA, with the backbones on the inside. This seemed plausible, and Watson and Crick explored that possibility.

Watson attended a lecture that was given by Rosalind Franklin in November. He had been learning crystallography but still did not under-stand all the details. Crick had often chided him for trusting his memory rather than taking notes—something Watson had done for years. This time, he misunderstood something Franklin said during her talk. As a result, the first Watson-Crick model was wrong.

Unaware of their mistakes, they invited Wilkins, Franklin, and two other scientists to view their three-stranded helical model with the phosphates in the center. The others did not hesitate to point out its flaws. There was still no proof that DNA was a helix, said Franklin. Also, the water content was wrong—it was eight molecules per nucleotide, not four molecules per lattice point.

Watson took the blame for the mistakes, later writing, "We were in trouble because I did not know enough of the crystallographic jargon. Particularly unfortunate was my failure to be able to report exactly the water content of the DNA samples upon which Rosy [Rosalind Franklin] had done her measurements."[9]

Crick felt responsible, too: "We tried to make a model which balanced the positive and negative charges. This was completely wrong because, in fact, there is a lot of water there. I did not know enough chemistry to know that things like sodium are highly likely to be hydrated anyway. Otherwise, I would have picked up the mistake. It was not only that Watson made the mistake but that I did not notice it, which is equally blameworthy. So it was a complete waste of time."[10] Crick also felt that his inexperience in building models kept him from noticing their early errors.

Watson and Crick suggested that they all collaborate on discovering the structure of DNA, but the King's College scientists did not agree. The senior scientists at the Cavendish discussed the situation and decided that King's

College would focus on DNA. Crick was told to return to his protein research, while Watson would study plant viruses. Watson and Crick gave the King's College group the molds they had used as model-components, but no one there tried that approach.

"By this time neither of us really wanted to look at our model," Watson remembered. "All its glamor had vanished, and the crudely improvised phosphorus atoms gave no hint that they would ever neatly fit into something of value."[11] Uncertain what to try next, they took a break from model-building.

However, they did not lose interest in DNA. Crick did some thinking about how helical molecules (a type of macromolecule) might be expected to behave. (His work on that topic eventually led to a scientific paper, published in a prominent journal the next year.) Eager to learn more, Watson borrowed Crick's copy of *The Chemical Bond* so often that he received a copy of his own that Christmas of 1951. It was signed, "To Jim from Francis."

Watson's holidays were brightened by a visit from his sister Elizabeth. She had been traveling throughout Europe and joined him in Scotland, at the home of one of his friends. He returned to Cambridge to find a letter about the status of his fellowship, which had remained uncertain since he left Denmark. The letter said that he had lost his fellowship and been given another,

"By this time, neither of us really wanted to look at our model," Watson remembered.

but for only eight months. Fortunately, Watson had saved a little money that he could use if nothing else turned up. He fully intended to stay at the Cavendish.

He and Francis Crick decided to rethink what they had done so far and make a fresh start on DNA. At the same time, they feared they would not be invited to hear about progress made in the King's College lab. Early in 1952, while Crick studied hemoglobin, Watson worked on x-ray diffractions of the tobacco mosaic virus. Instead of DNA, this virus contained RNA. The x-ray diffraction pictures of the virus suggested a helical pattern. Excited, Watson showed them to Crick, who came up with several possible formations the helix might take. Watson was frustrated that he knew so little about helical theory. He knew Crick could help with the mathematics in his spare time, but he did some extra reading on his own. He also began taking a series of x-ray photographs, and, after more than a month of practice, had developed some "halfway presentable pictures."[12]

That May, Linus Pauling was scheduled to speak at a conference in London. Watson and Crick assumed he would visit King's College and examine the x-ray photographs of DNA. However, Pauling was prevented from traveling when the U.S. State Department revoked his passport on political grounds. Because of his efforts to ban nuclear weapons, Pauling was among those

branded as a "Communist" during the Cold War
era. During this period, paranoia about "trai-
tors" in the U.S. government was rampant and
numerous citizens were forced to testify before
Senator Joseph McCarthy's committee on
"un-American activities." Watson and Crick
found the government's action distasteful and
unfair to Pauling.

At about this time, Watson read a letter
from Alfred Hershey describing some exciting
research in America. Hershey and a colleague,
Martha Chase, had shown that, when a virus
enters a bacteria cell, its DNA, rather than protein molecules, enters and then changes the
appearance of the bacteria. Watson and others
saw this as proof that DNA controls heredity.

At a Paris meeting, Watson was cheered
when Max Delbrück told him he had arranged
for a new fellowship, from the National Polio
Foundation, set to start in September 1952.
Watson described what he and Crick had been
doing and told of his virus studies. By now,
the State Department had reinstated Linus
Pauling's passport, and he was at the meeting
to discuss his "alpha helix" structure of proteins.
Later, Ava Helen Pauling told Watson that their
son Peter would be studying at Cambridge the
following year.

Watson vacationed in the Italian Alps that
August, while Crick spent a month giving lectures on biophysics in Brazil. When they both

returned to England, Watson was absorbed by some new discoveries about bacteria and showed less interest in DNA, to Crick's disappointment.

Crick was now re-examining Chargaff's rules about the proportions of base chemicals in DNA. He wrote a paper theorizing that alpha helices are found in coiled coils—that is, the coils themselves form denser coils as they are packed together in cells. When he was sure his mathematical calculations on the subject were correct, Crick sent his paper to the prestigious science journal, *Nature*.

Two important events soon brought Watson and Crick back to DNA. New photographs from Rosalind Franklin indicated that DNA might be a double-stranded helix, with a sugar-phosphate backbone on the outside. And early in 1953, when Peter Pauling arrived in England, he showed Watson and Crick a paper that described his father's idea about the structure of DNA. The two scientists saw that Pauling's model could not be accurate. At the time, said Watson, "I knew we were still in the game."[13]

Chapter 3: Notes

1. Crick, 64; Judson, 111.
2. Judson, 112.
3. Watson, 50.
4. Judson, 112.
5. Crick, 64.
6. Quoted in Richard Olby, 247.
7. Quoted in Judson, 116.
8. Crick, 33.
9. Watson, 76.
10. Quoted in Richard Olby, 360–61.
11. Watson, 96.
12. Watson, 115.
13. Watson, 161.

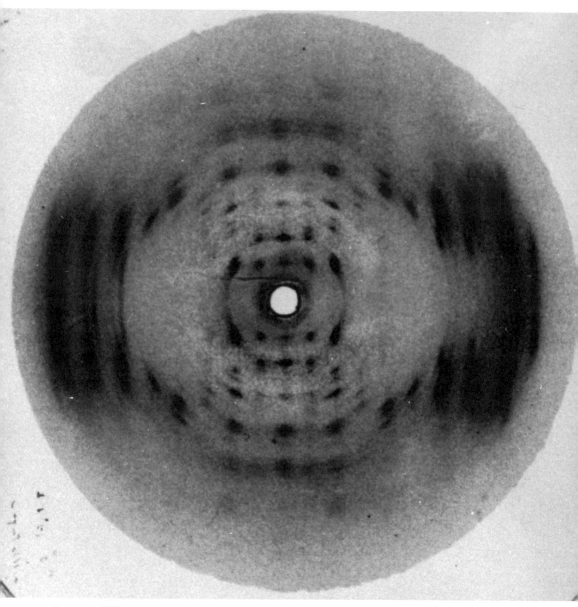

An x-ray diffraction of a DNA molecule, taken by Rosalind Franklin.

Solving an
Age-Old Puzzle

"We have discovered the secret of life."

—*Francis Crick*

In the early months of 1953, Watson and Crick were busy, both inside and outside the lab. The Cricks were settling into a new home—an interesting old, narrow house not far from the Cavendish. Watson had also moved, to a new room at Clare College on the Cambridge grounds. He was happy to be on campus and especially appreciated the garden.

The two men continued to think and talk about DNA, off and on. While working on viruses, Watson considered the idea that DNA might serve as a template on which RNA chains could be made. He later wrote, "On the wall above my desk I taped up a paper sheet saying DNA—RNA—protein."[1]

Yet neither man came up with a strong idea for a new model. Sometimes Watson and Crick spent whole lunches together without mentioning DNA, and then the subject would surface during an after-lunch walk. When feeling inspired, they manipulated the pieces of their three-dimensional models. Watson later wrote that at times when these efforts seemed futile, Crick gravitated back to his hemoglobin studies. "Several times I carried on alone for a half hour or so, but without Francis' reassuring chatter my inability to think in three dimensions became all too apparent," he said.[2]

Early in 1953, Rosalind Franklin announced that, in a few months, she would move to a different lab. (She and Maurice Wilkins had never gotten along well.) Wilkins told Watson that Franklin would not be continuing DNA research after she left. She had decided to concentrate her attention on the tobacco mosaic virus, and she went on to make important discoveries about its structure. Before she left, she wrapped up her DNA studies and summarized the findings so they could be published and shared with other scientists.

In February 1953, Wilkins met Watson for dinner and showed him some photographs of DNA that had been taken at King's College late in 1952. Franklin's skill in preparing DNA samples under controlled humidity, along with the fine camera equipment at the lab, had yielded high-quality results. The pictures supported a theory Franklin had that the bases *A, C, T,* and *G*—were in the center of the DNA molecule, with the backbone on the outside.

As he rode home that night, Watson sketched the pattern of DNA he remembered from the photographs. The next day, he showed it to Crick and suggested that they attempt a new model, with two chains—a double helix instead of a triple-stranded one. He offered new ideas about where the chemical pattern might repeat itself along the helix, and the two came up with new estimates of its diameter.

Soon, the machinist at the lab was making new models of phosphorus atoms and *purines* (the chemical group that includes the larger

Watson said that he often "carried on alone ... but without Francis' reassuring chatter my inability to think in three dimensions became all too apparent."

bases, adenine and guanine) and *pyrimidines* (the group that includes the smaller bases, cytosine and thymine). Each of these four bases has a different shape because each is made up of different atoms with different chemical bonds.

When these metal pieces were ready, Watson developed some accurate scale models of the sugar and phosphate groups. But once again, the two scientists faced obstacles when they tried to fit the pieces together. For his part, Watson did not like the idea of moving the backbone of the molecule from the center to the outside, knowing that this configuration could lead to "an almost infinite number of models...."[3]

Together they tried new models, often with Watson moving the pieces as Crick did calculations. At other times, they worked separately. Watson tended to go to the lab early each morning, when he could work alone before anyone else arrived. While Watson took afternoon breaks to play tennis, Crick tried out his ideas.

Their chief problem at the time was where to place the bases—the purines and pyrimidines (*A, G, C,* and *T*). Although there was room to place two bases between the sugar molecules that lay across from each other in the helix, the two purines were too large to fit inside the strands. Likewise, the two pyrimidines were too small. Not only did Watson and Crick have to place the bases correctly, they also had to decide how far apart they should be.

Once again, they consulted chemistry texts and tried out various ideas on paper. While sketching what he called "fused rings of adenine,"[4] Watson considered locating hydrogen bonds at certain points on the molecule. Both men thought that idea made sense chemically, but the resulting model did not work.

Fortunately, Jerry Donohue, an American crystallographer and expert on hydrogen bonds, was then working at the Cavendish. He told Watson and Crick that they had chosen the wrong chemical forms of guanine and thymine in constructing their model. The photographs in the books they had read were incorrect, said Donohue. He believed these bases took what chemists called the *keto* form, rather than the *enol* form, which was what Watson and Crick had been using.

Donohue's suggestion was important information. It affected the location of atoms in the bases, and the bonds those atoms would form with other atoms in the molecule. Since they had no metal models of these new forms for their large model, Watson made a new set of bases to scale out of cardboard. With the keto forms of guanine and thymine, hydrogen bonds were chemically possible. But there was now a large gap in size between a pair of purines (*A* and *G*) and a pair of pyrimidines (*C* and *T*). As they had it, these pairs would not fit properly within the helical structure.

Together, they tried new models, often with Watson moving the pieces as Crick did calculations.

In late February came another breakthrough. Francis Crick later wrote, "The key discovery was Jim's determination of the exact nature of the two base pairs (A with T, G with C)."[5] It was an idea they may have discussed previously, Crick recalled, although he was not sure when they had first talked about this type of pairing or the reasons for discarding the idea.[6] Using the cardboard cutouts one Saturday morning, Watson found that adenine could form two hydrogen bonds with the pyrimidine thymine, if placed together the right way. When A was paired with C or G, parts of the atoms did not fit properly. Furthermore, the model of the A-T pair was congruent to the C-G pair; they would fit neatly into the backbones of the molecule.

Now that Donohue's insights had made hydrogen bonds possible, Crick agreed that pairing purines with pyrimidines was a good idea. He also pointed out that the way in which the bases were attached to their sugars meant that the two backbones of the molecule must run in opposite directions. Watson felt elated that a final answer might be near: "It seemed almost unbelievable that the DNA structure was solved, that the answer was incredibly exciting, and that our names would be associated with the double helix as Pauling's was with the alpha helix."[7] With their puzzle finally solved, Crick was heard to say, "We have discovered the secret of life."[8]

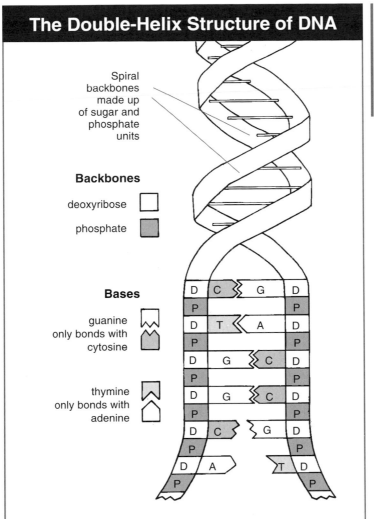

In *The Double Helix,* Watson described what happened after the machine shop finished making the metal pieces they had requested: "In about an hour I had arranged the atoms in positions which satisfied both the x-ray data and the laws of stereochemistry. The resulting helix was right-handed with the two chains running in opposite directions. Only one person can easily

"It seemed almost unbelievable that the DNA structure was solved."

play with a model, and so Francis did not try to check my work until I backed away and said that I thought everything fitted."[9]

Then Crick stepped forward. Watson watched anxiously as his partner frowned a few times while moving first to one part, then to another piece of the model, checking the atoms and the points where they made contact. They were both relieved when Crick agreed that everything looked correct. With the bases paired *A* to *T* and *C* to *G*, they had achieved the chemical ratio of adenine, thymine, guanine, and cytosine that Chargaff had originally calculated for DNA molecules. In this version, each pair was held together by two hydrogen bonds. Donohue was consulted again and also thought that this design made sense.

After eighteen months of starts and stops and trial and error, James Watson and Francis Crick had constructed a model that agreed with the available data about the DNA molecule. It took the form of a double helix, in which two intertwined strands climbed upward, like a spiral staircase. The backbone (frame) of the molecule had sugar groups alternating with the phosphates. These sugar-phosphate chains formed the spirals. The coil made a complete turn after every ten phosphate groups. The "stairs" were the four bases—*A* paired with *T, C* paired with *G*—joined to the sides at right angles. These base pairs were equal in length. Their model was not only scientifically plausible, they considered it quite "pretty" in appearance.[10] The two strands of the helix were complementary in their components. For example, if one strand held a series of bases like this: *A-G-C-A-C-C*, the strand opposite it would have *T-C-G-T-G-G*.

Of course, the two scientists wanted to share their results with the world as soon as possible, but first they wanted to feel more sure of their model. Clearly, this great new finding would have a tremendous impact on the work of DNA researchers around the world. Before making any announcement, Watson and Crick had to check over all their notes and measurements carefully.

Crick arrived at the lab first the next morning and began tightening various parts of the model and rearranging the ring stands that supported it. With a compass and ruler, he took precise measurements, based on what the x-ray photographs had shown about the probable distances among various atoms in the DNA molecule. When Watson arrived, he helped to hold the model in place while his mind drifted to the exciting letters he would soon be able to write to colleagues.

Although the structure seemed correct, the two scientists spent several days rechecking their measurements. When all seemed well, the pair invited William L. Bragg, Kendrew, Perutz, and others to see it. The observers agreed that the model made sense in terms of gene replication. Bragg advised them to have the lab's top chemists evaluate it as well.

When Maurice Wilkins finally came to the Cavendish, he said, "I think you're a couple of rogues but you well may have something. I like the idea."[11] Wilkins offered to help them verify their work. Watson was relieved, for he had feared that Wilkins might resent having to share the glory of the discovery. After all, the King's College scientists had worked long and hard on the DNA puzzle themselves.[12] A few days later, Wilkins informed them that he and Rosalind Franklin believed that their most recent photographs supported the Watson-Crick model. He suggested that he, Franklin, Watson, and Crick submit three articles about their results to the leading science journal *Nature*.

Watson had previously scheduled a week-long visit to a laboratory in Paris and decided to make the trip as planned, although Crick thought they should keep working on their model. While in Paris, Watson learned that new chemical studies on phage DNA supported their DNA model. When he returned, Crick had assembled an additional model. This one showed the DNA molecule in a different form, the one it took when the fibers contained less water and were therefore shorter.

As various people came to see the double helix, Francis Crick enthusiastically told them about the structure and its biochemical implications. As might be expected, there was much excitement in the lab. When Rosalind Franklin visited, she, Watson, and Crick had their first really enjoyable conversations about DNA. Watson had come to appreciate Franklin as a first-rate scientist who must have faced many obstacles while working in a field dominated by men. He was glad to see her increased respect for their work and for their use of scientific models.

During March, Watson and Crick prepared a 900-word article about their findings. They disagreed over certain points as they wrote it. Crick wanted to say more about the genetic implications of their DNA model, while Watson feared saying too much and possibly being proven wrong. In the end, they compromised and mentioned some of their theories. On a Saturday afternoon, they enlisted the help of Watson's sister, Elizabeth, to type the paper. Watson later recalled that as she typed, he and Crick told her "that she was participating in perhaps the most famous event in biology since Darwin's book."[13]

In a letter to his son Michael, who was away at school, Crick wrote, '[The pairing of the bases] is like a code. If you are given one set of letters, you can write down the others. Now we believe that the DNA *is* a code. That is, the order of the bases (the letters) makes one gene

Crick explained to his son that the pairing of the bases "is like a code. If you are given one set of letters, you can write down the others."

different from another gene (just as one page of print is different from another)."[14]

On April 25, 1953, Watson and Crick's brief article appeared in *Nature*. It began in a low-keyed manner: "We wish to suggest a structure for the salt of deoxyribonucleic acid (DNA). This structure has novel features which are of considerable biological interest." The article went on to say that the double-helix pattern "suggests a possible copying mechanism for the genetic material." During DNA replication, the helix unwinds and splits apart into two single strands. Base material inside the cell nucleus then attaches to the appropriate points on the open DNA chain, resulting in two identical molecules. Later, observers said, "in one page [Watson and Crick] revolutionized biology."[15]

Five weeks after their initial article, Watson and Crick published a second paper in *Nature*, discussing the further genetic implications of the double helix. In the meantime, other scientists analyzed their first article and diagrams, and not everyone agreed with them. Some scientists contended that DNA was not a double helix at all, but was instead composed of two side-by-side, separate chains. This theory was not widely accepted, but a few details of the Watson-Crick model turned out to be incorrect. Linus Pauling suggested that there were three, and not two, hydrogen bonds in the guanine-cytosine pair, and Watson and Crick both agreed with his reasoning. Also, the bases were located a bit too far from the axis of the molecule. Nonetheless, the basic model held up to the intense scrutiny that followed.

They had made a major discovery, but the two scientists really regarded it as a beginning rather than an end. Now that the double helix was in view, the next challenge—and an even more complicated one—was to find out exactly what it did and how. This quest would again involve Watson and Crick, sometimes together and at other times separately, as well as numerous other scientists.

Watson and Crick had concluded that the sequence of the base chemicals across the DNA helix carries information that determines how proteins are made inside a cell. Yet protein synthesis (the process by which the different amino acids are made into proteins) takes place outside the cell nucleus, while the genes are inside it. They concluded that RNA, found mostly in the *cytoplasm* (part of the cell outside the nucleus), must play a key role. As a result, RNA and protein synthesis became their new focus. Here, Crick's background in protein molecules was a great asset.

Although Francis Crick was now a well-known scientist, he was still by no means wealthy. He and Odile did manage to save enough money to buy a house that was adjacent to theirs and partially joined the two buildings

Crick remained
very interested
in showing that
the DNA "code"
is universal—the
same in all organ-
isms, whether
human, plant,
or animal.

together. By then, the Crick family included two young daughters, Gabrielle and Jacqueline. The house was dubbed "The Golden Helix" (a popular nickname for DNA), and Crick placed a brass helix above the door.

In the fall of 1953, Watson left England for southern California. He had been named a Senior Research Fellow at the California Institute of Technology, where he studied RNA. Using x-ray crytallography, he added to the growing body of knowledge about how RNA works with DNA to make proteins inside cells.

Crick also left the Cavendish during the year of 1953-54 to make his first trip to the United States. At the Brooklyn Polytechnic in New York, he took part in the Protein Structure Project. During this time, he remained very interested in showing that the DNA "code" is *universal*—the same in all organisms, whether human, plant, or animal.

During the summer of 1954, he and Watson joined other scientists at Wood's Hole in Massachusetts, often discussing protein synthesis and other DNA-related topics. That summer, he also came up with theories about how a single mutant in a gene, by changing just one amino acid of the twenty that exist, could alter the protein. One scientist at Wood's Hole suggested that they form an RNA Tie Club, to include twenty top scientists working on RNA, one for each type of amino acid. Each member, including Watson and Crick, received a necktie featuring a picture of "their" amino-acid chain. Although the group did not meet formally, they sometimes exchanged articles they had written about new theories. Their unusual ties also made good conversation pieces.

In 1955, Crick was working on the structure of collagen (the proteins that make up claws, fingernails, and feathers, among other tissues). That same year, he and Watson again teamed up at Cambridge to study the structure of viruses. After they completed this work and published their findings in 1956, Watson returned to the United States, this time to stay. He became a professor in the biology department at Harvard University in Cambridge, Massachusetts. The laboratory that Watson began to develop at Harvard would train a number of prominent molecular biologists in the years that followed.

For his part, Crick continued to work on the genetic code, a field in which he became a world leader. He studied the order of the bases in the DNA molecule and theorized that the number, order, and types of bases in the DNA molecule contain the information needed to pass on traits from parent organisms to their offspring. Although DNA has the same chemical proportions in all organisms, the possible combinations and arrangements of the four bases along the helical strands are infinite. This fact explains why life on the planet is so diverse.

More exciting news about DNA came in 1956. Arthur Kornberg, a biochemist working at New York University, had duplicated DNA in a test tube. With the Watson-Crick DNA model for guidance, Kornberg had isolated the enzyme he thought a cell must use in making DNA. In a test tube he combined DNA with the bases *A, T, C,* and *G,* along with this enzyme. The result was that, for the first known time, genetic material had actually been made outside a living cell. Kornberg and his colleague Severo Ochoa, who had duplicated RNA, jointly received a Nobel Prize in Medicine in 1959.

These findings stimulated the already vibrant field of molecular biology. People predicted that scientists would find ways to use DNA as a sort of genetic "blueprint" to develop new forms of life in the lab. As new findings were made, they confirmed the validity of Watson and Crick's 1953 model and theories.

Still, not everyone praised the two scientists. Critics argued that they had merely stumbled upon the correct structure of DNA. Crick later said that they deserved to be given credit for their persistence and effort: "It's true that by blundering about we stumbled on gold, but the fact remains that we were looking for gold.... We could not at all see what the answer was, but we considered it so important that we were determined to think about it long and hard, from any relevant point of view. Practically nobody else was prepared to make such an intellectual investment, since it involved not only studying genetics, biochemistry, chemistry, and physical chemistry (including x-ray diffraction—and who was prepared to learn that?) but also sorting out the essential gold from the dross."[16]

In 1962, members of the Nobel Committee agreed that James Watson and Francis Crick had struck scientific gold. The two men—then both at Harvard University, where Watson was a professor and Crick was a visiting professor in biophysics—received the gratifying news that they had been awarded the highly coveted Nobel Prize.

Chapter 4: Notes

1. Watson, 153.
2. Watson, 155.
3. Watson, 177.
4. Crick, 184.
5. Crick, 65.
6. Judson, 172.
7. Watson, 198.
8. Quoted in Judson, 175.
9. Watson, 100.
10. Watson, 205.
11. Olby, 417.
12. Watson, 209.
13. Watson, 221–22.
14. Judson, 178.
15. Portugal and Cohen, 263.
16. Crick, 74–75.

Crick and Watson speak with fellow Nobel Prize winners at the ceremony in
Stockholm, 1962.

After the Golden Helix

"Good science as a way of life is difficult…

we must thus believe strongly in our ideas,

often to the point where

they may seem tiresome."

—*James Watson*

On December 10, 1962, in Stockholm, Sweden, James Watson, Francis Crick, and Maurice Wilkins accepted the Nobel Prize for physiology or medicine. Many science historians believe that Rosalind Franklin would also have shared in the award had she not died at age thirty-seven in 1958. Also at the ceremony were their Cavendish colleagues, John Kendrew and Max Perutz, who received the Nobel Prize in chemistry.

That evening, the Nobel laureates were honored at a ball and banquet where they made brief speeches. Watson called receiving a Nobel Prize "the second greatest moment of my life" (the first being the discovery of the DNA structure). Near the end of his speech, he said, "Good science as a way of life is difficult...We must thus believe strongly in our ideas, often to the point where they may seem tiresome and bothersome and even arrogant to our colleagues. I know many people, at least when I was young, who thought I was quite unbearable. Some also thought Maurice was very strange, and others, including myself, thought Francis was at times difficult."[1]

After leaving Sweden, Watson and John Kendrew went to Geneva, Switzerland, to visit CERN (the international nuclear physics research center). They met with Leo Szilard, a well-known physicist-turned-biologist, and agreed to help him develop a new international research lab for biological projects. With support from Watson and other biologists, EMBO (the European Molecular Biology Organization) would become a reality in 1979, with John Kendrew as its first director. Located in Heidelberg, Germany, with branches in Hamburg, Germany, and Grenoble, France, EMBO has funded the work of many scientists.

After the Nobel ceremonies, Francis Crick returned to his work with the National Medical Research Council Laboratory of Molecular Biology in Cambridge. By the late 1960s, he was one of the leading authorities on "cracking" the DNA code. Along these research lines, he continued to study the synthesis of proteins. Both he and Watson wrote scientific papers during these years. Both regularly received scientific honors, sometimes jointly, and they were in demand as guest lecturers on subjects relating to molecular biology.

Still teaching at Harvard, Watson found time to write a personal account of the discovery of the structure of the DNA molecule. He showed Crick excerpts of the book while he was working on it. Crick's first impressions were that Watson had focused too much on the personalities and relationships of the people involved. He feared some of those mentioned in the book might be offended and that the general public would have little interest in the scientific material.

Cold Spring Harbor Laboratory, in Long Island, New York.

Despite Crick's misgivings, *The Double Helix,* was published in 1968. It became a best-seller. As time went on, Crick's attitude toward the book mellowed. He said it was well written and much like a good detective novel while still including a fair amount of science.

That same year, Watson was named director of Cold Spring Harbor Laboratory, a biological station on Long Island, New York. For years, Watson had attended meetings there and enjoyed the way in which scientists studied and exchanged ideas. He once told an interviewer, "It is the most interesting place in the world if you're interested in biology."[2] As director, Watson set up postgraduate programs in cell biochemistry, including DNA studies. He also turned his attention to cancer research, organizing

studies of tumor virology and the role of genes
in the development of cancer. In addition, he
remained at Harvard, where he taught advanced
courses in viruses, among other things.

Watson must have been pleased in 1969
when new honors came to three men who had
inspired him in his earlier days. The founders of
the American phage group—Salvador Luria,
Alfred Hershey, and Max Delbrück—won the
Nobel Prize for physiology or medicine.

A few years later, Francis Crick, with whom
Watson was in regular contact, moved to the
United States. Since 1962, Crick had been
affiliated with The Salk Institute for Biological
Studies, based in La Jolla, California. The institute had been founded by the renowned doctor,
Jonas Salk. He was the medical researcher and
expert on viruses who developed the first effec-
tive vaccine against polio. While organizing his
institute, Salk had consulted Crick and other
scientists. Prominent thinkers from various fields
went to the institute to study and conduct various kinds of research. Crick had spent time there
himself, and in 1976, he finally agreed to come
as a resident distinguished research professor.
Crick resigned from the Medical Research
Council, and he and Odile moved to La Jolla,
California. Crick took great pleasure in the
natural beauty of his new surroundings, over-
looking the Pacific Ocean and near both desert
and mountain areas.

Along with a new home, Crick had a new scientific interest. Years before as a student, he had been fascinated by the brain. He had read widely in this area and enjoyed meeting neurobiologists (scientists who study the structure and function of the brain). Now he wanted to study these matters for himself, focusing on consciousness. Crick planned to start by developing theories about the visual systems of mammals. Crick said that understanding how neurons (nerve cells) operate with various chemical processes in the body may show us "exactly how these activities give us our vivid picture of the world and of ourselves and also allow us to act."[3] His book *The Astonishing Hypothesis*, published in 1993, further describes his ideas.

While his former partner shifted to a new area of research, Watson had left research behind to write and develop programs that would train and inspire other scientists. In 1981, he and John Tooze published *The DNA Story: A Documentary History of Gene Cloning*. He would later help to write a college-level textbook, *Molecular Biology of the Cell*, and *Recombinant DNA: A Short Course*, both first published in 1983. By this time, Watson had also married. He and his wife, Elizabeth Lewis, were now raising two sons, Rufus and Duncan.

As Watson and Crick moved on with their busy personal lives and new professional challenges, others had not forgotten their thrilling discovery of more than twenty years earlier. A film about their collaboration on DNA was produced by the British Broadcasting Company (BBC) in the 1980s. In Great Britain, the film was broadcast under the title *Life Story*; in the United States, it was called *Double Helix.*

Progress in genetic research had been great since the 1950s. New methods of analyzing the sequence of DNA on chromosomes had enabled scientists to locate specific genes. As these researchers realized that it might be possible to identify every gene found in human beings, a program called the Human Genome Initiative was formed. It was begun in 1988 under the National Institutes of Health, with James Watson as associate director. Between 1990 and 1992, Watson served as director of the project. Because of the vast number of genes involved (possibly 100,000), Watson suggested that nations throughout the world pool their scientific resources to tackle the genome project.

During these years, Watson also remained director of the Cold Spring Harbor Laboratory. By the 1990s, about four thousand scientists a year were taking part in the educational and research activities at the laboratory.

The genome project in which Watson played a key role is just one of many outgrowths of the 1953 discovery of the double helix. The field of molecular biology has exploded, steadily uncovering more secrets of life. There are perhaps 100

In the 1990s, Watson became involved in the Human Genome Initiative, which set out to chart and identify every gene found in human beings.

trillion cells in a human body (about 1 million per every square inch of skin). Each cell contains some 100,000 different genes. As Watson and Crick had once surmised, most plant and animal cells contain an entire set of genes for their species. Learning about DNA, the material that makes up these thousands of genes and directs cell growth, has obviously been tremendously important.

Better instrumentation has made it possible to see more details of DNA. But pictures of DNA fail to convey its phenomenal physical capacity. One author describes DNA strands as being "so narrow and tightly coiled…that all the genes in all the cells in a human body would fit into a box the size of an ice cube. Yet if all this DNA were unwound and joined together, the string could stretch from the earth to the sun and back more than 400 times."[4]

Building on the work done by Watson, Crick, and others, scientists have learned more about how DNA directs the chemical machinery of a cell to make a specific protein. In this process, DNA is used as a pattern to make RNA, which in turn, is used to direct the synthesis of a string of amino acids, or protein. The protein molecule then leaves the cell to perform important functions in the body.

In 1954, Vernon Ingram, who worked with Francis Crick at the Cavendish, found a way to detect how one amino acid might be substituted for another in proteins. This helped others to study specific diseases. In 1959, Ingram found that an error in one amino acid of the protein that makes up red blood cells results in the disease sickle-cell anemia.

After Arthur Kornberg and his group duplicated DNA in the lab in 1956, other scientists tried to figure out how DNA was divided into certain genes and exactly how it coded its instructions to the body. They especially wanted to know how the order of the nucleotides (repeating sequences of bases) in a DNA molecule were coded for different kinds of proteins. This information was needed if scientists were to undertake genetic engineering—finding and changing specific genes on the DNA strands.

"Cracking the DNA code" absorbed many scientists, including Crick and others at the Cavendish; a group led by Spanish-born Severo Ochoa at New York University; Gobind Khorana; and Marshall Nirenberg and his colleagues at the National Institutes of Health. For his discoveries about the DNA code, Nirenberg won a Nobel Prize in 1968.

During the 1970s and 1980s, DNA research led to many practical applications in agriculture, medicine, and other technology-sensitive fields. Scientists used specific enzymes to cut and recombine segments of DNA in the chromosomes of various bacteria. New technology enabled researchers to remove DNA from different

In 1988, James Watson became the associate director of the Human Genome Initiative.

bacteria and then combine it with another to make—recombinant—DNA. The delicate process of moving genes to new places on chromosomes is called gene splicing. In 1982, human insulin, the hormone that regulates sugar metabolism in the body, was made using recombinant DNA methods. New types of tomatoes and other plants have also been created through genetic engineering.

In recent years, scientists have found better ways to analyze the DNA in chromosomes. DNA testing is now used to analyze blood found at crime scenes and to establish the likelihood of paternity. Scientists can also diagnose several hundred genetic abnormalities before birth, including sickle-cell anemia, Tay-Sach's Disease, and Down Syndrome.

Knowing that DNA "tells" a cell how long to grow and how to repair some damage, scientists are seeking new ways to treat diseases and slow the aging process. They are especially eager to learn more about retroviruses. A retrovirus is composed of RNA rather than DNA and replicates itself by reading the DNA code in reverse. The potentially deadly HIV (human immunodeficiency) virus is a retrovirus, thought to cause AIDS (acquired immunodeficiency syndrome) by weakening or destroying the body's disease-fighting immune system.

Some genetic breakthroughs are quite controversial and have provoked heated ethical debates about where to "draw the line." How much information is too much? Should people be tested for genetic diseases even when there is no cure? Do humans have the right to control life-forms with these powerful new biotechnologies? What if someone uses DNA technology for corrupt purposes, such as germ warfare, or to develop so-called "superior" or "perfect" people? Various countries have developed codes of ethics and laws to deal with these issues.

Apart and together—as researchers, teachers, writers, or administrators—James Watson and Francis Crick have propelled and witnessed these strides in molecular biology. And the results of their partnership have sparked untold new developments. When they first came together, the two men contributed different types of related and valuable knowledge—Crick in crystallography and physics, Watson in phage genetics and biology. Yet, their collaboration was more than the sum of their individual skills.

Both scientists have reminisced about the elements that made their partnership flourish. For one thing, they agreed on the problem to be addressed and were willing to devote themselves wholeheartedly to solving it. Crick viewed the closeness in their ages as an asset, saying that if one of them had been much older than the other, they might have felt a need to be too polite to each other—"the end of all good collaboration in science."[5]

Watson and Crick pose with their model at a symposium held in 1990.

In his book *What Mad Pursuit?*, Crick later wrote that, in his opinion, a collaboration like theirs would require people to "be perfectly candid." He said, "If, for example, I had some idea, which…was going off [on] a tangent, Watson would tell me in no uncertain terms… this was nonsense, and vice versa."[6] Crick said that such collaboration "helps jolt one out of false assumptions. A typical example was Jim's initial insistence that the phosphates must be on the inside of the structure…. 'Why not,' I said to Jim one evening, build models with the phosphates on the outside.'" As they continued to debate that revolutionary concept, it forced them to pay more attention to the structure and composition of the bases, which led to other key ideas in solving the correct structure.[7]

The two men were both skeptical of the theories and assumptions that had already been offered by other researchers about DNA. They knew that some of their predecessors had followed the wrong leads because they relied on evidence that was later proven false. Crick recalled, "every bit of experimental evidence we had got at any one time we were prepared to throw away, because we said it may be misleading…not only can data be wrong in science, it can be misleading. There isn't such a thing as a hard fact when you're trying to discover something. It's only afterwards that the facts become hard."[8]

Besides their own successful working relationship, the partners felt fortunate that Jerry Donohue had been at Cambridge at the right time. Watson wrote, "If he had not been at Cambridge, I might still have been pumping for a like-with-like structure. Maurice [Wilkins] in a lab [without] structural chemists, did not have anyone about to tell him that all the textbook pictures were wrong."[9]

Crick later wrote about the moment when Watson first realized how to pair the bases in the molecule: "In a sense, Jim's discovery was luck, but then most discoveries have an element of luck in them. The more important point is that Jim was looking for something significant and immediately recognized the significance of the correct pairs when he hit upon them by chance—chance favors the prepared mind. This episode also demonstrates that play is often important in research."[10]

In the 1970s, Francis Crick said, "If Watson had never come to Cambridge, who would have discovered the structure? More important, how long would it have taken? After all, the structure was there waiting to be discovered—Watson and I did not invent it. It seems to me unlikely that either of us would have done it separately."[11]

As both Watson and Crick have admitted, the answer to the DNA puzzle was there, waiting to be discovered. The double helix had existed on the planet for perhaps billions of years before their discovery of its amazing structure brought it to light. Since that time, the work produced by their scientific partnership has set off a chain of new and incredible discoveries. It has also raised wondrous—as well as a few potentially terrifying—possibilities for the human race as scientists learn better how to manipulate the most essential code of life.

Chapter 5: Notes

1. Quoted in Judson, 581.
2. Judson, 44.
3. Crick, 154.
4. Rick Gore, et al., "The New Biology," *National Geographic,* vol. 150, no. 3 (September 1976: 356-57.
5. Crick, 13.
6. Ibid.
7. Crick, 70.
8. Quoted in Judson, 113–14.
9. Watson, 209.
10. Crick, 66.
11. Richard Olby, *The Path to the Double Helix,* vi.

Bibliography

Crick, Francis. *What Mad Pursuit?* New York: Basic Books, 1988.

Dickson, David. "Watson Floats Up a Plan to Carve Up the Genome." *Science*, May 5, 1989, 621–622.

Dunn, L. C., Editor. *Genetics in the Twentieth Century: Essays on the Progress of Genetics in Its First Fifty Years.* New York: Macmillan, 1951.

Golob, Richard, and Brus, Eric. *The Almanac of Science and Technology: What's New and What's Known.* New York: Harcourt, 1990.

Gore, Rick, et al. "The New Biology." *National Geographic*, vol. 150, no. 3 (September 1976), 355–399.

Gunther, S. Stent and Richard Calendar. *Molecular Genetics: An Introductory Narrative.* 2nd Edition. San Francisco: W. H. Freeman, 1978.

Horgan, John. "Can Science Explain Consciousness?" *Scientific American.* July 1994, 88–94.

Judson, Horace. *The Eighth Day of Creation.* New York: Simon and Schuster, 1979.

Olby, Richard. *The Path to the Double Helix.* Seattle: University of Washington Press, 1974.

Pauling, Linus. "Molecular Basis of Biological Specificity." *Nature*, April 26, 1974, 769–771.

Portugal, Franklin H., and Cohen, Jack S. *A Century of DNA: A History of the Discovery of the Structure and Function of the Genetic Substance.* Cambridge, Mass.: The MIT Press, 1977.

"The Salt Institute for Biological Studies: Profile of a Unique Research Center." Unpublished Faculty brochure. La Jolla, CA: (n.d.).

Seidler, Ned, and Gore, Rick. "Seven Giants Who Led the Way." *National Geographic*, vol 150, no. 3 (September 1976), 401–407.

Serafini, Anthony. *Linus Pauling: A Man and His Science*. New York: Paragon House, 1989.

Shorter, Edward. *The Health Century*. New York: Doubleday, 1987.

Watson, James Dewey. *The Double Helix*. New York: Atheneum, 1968.

Watson, James Dewey, and Tooze, John. *The DNA Story: A Documentary History of Gene Cloning*. San Francisco: W. H. Freeman, 1981.

Weaver, Robert F. "Changing Life's Genetic Blueprint." *National Geographic*. Vol. 166, No. 6 (December 1984), 818–833.

Williams, Trevor I. *Science: A History of Discovery in the Twentieth Century*. Oxford: Oxford University Press, 1990.

Chronology

1600s Living cells are looked at under a microscope for the first time.

1859 Charles Darwin's book *The Origin of the Species* proposes that all life evolved from very simple cells.

1865 Gregor Mendel publishes his studies regarding heredity in pea plants.

1869 Johann Friedrich Miescher discovers what would come to be known as DNA.

1902 Walter Stanborough Sutton discovers that chromosomes come in pairs.

1909 Wilhem Johannsen names hereditary units on chromosomes genes.

1915 *The Mechanism of Mendelian Heredity* is published, showing how certain traits are inherited.

June 8, 1916 Francis Harry Compton Crick is born in Northampton, England.

1922 RNA is found in an animal's pancreatic cells; DNA is found in plants.

April 6, 1928 James Watson is born in Chicago, Illinois.

1930 Crick wins a scholarship to Mill Hill School.

1937 Crick earns a physics degree from University College in London.

1940s Austrian-American biochemist Erwin Chargaff discovers that the amount of DNA in cells were equivalent for many organisms.

1940 Crick joins the British Admiralty Research Laboratory. He also marries Doreen Dodd and they have a son, Michael.

1943 *What Is Life?* by Austrian physicist Erwin Schrödinger is published. Watson enters the University of Chicago as a zoology major.

1947–1949 Crick works with Dr. Honor Fell at Strangeways Laboratory in Cambridge to learn more about biophysical techniques.

1947 Watson receives his bachelor degree. He enters the Indiana University to do graduate work in genetics.

1948 Watson visits Cold Spring Harbor Laboratory in New York.

1949 Crick meets and becomes friends with Maurice Wilkins. He also marries for the second time to Odile Speed. Crick goes to work at the Cavendish Laboratory in Cambridge to learn more about the character of protein molecules.

1950 Watson completes his doctoral thesis on the effects of x-rays on bacterial viruses. He goes to Copenhagen to study nucleic acids.

1951 James Watson arrives at Cavendish Laboratory and meets Francis Crick for the first time. Rosalind Franklin arrives at King's College Laboratory. British scientist Alexander Todd and his colleagues discover the makeup of the backbone of the DNA molecule.

Fall 1951 Watson and Crick begin work on their first DNA model.

1952 Watson receives a new fellowship from the National Polio Foundation to continue studies at Cavendish.

1953 Watson and Crick work on new models of DNA and build what they believe to be a correct DNA model. Crick receives his doctorate.

April 25—Watson and Crick publish their paper theorizing how DNA works in cell reproduction.

Fall Watson leaves England to become a Senior Research Fellow at California Institute of Technology.

1953–1954 Crick takes part in the Protein Structure Project at Brooklyn Polytechnic Institute.

1955 Crick works on the structure of collagen. Watson and Crick study the structure of viruses in Cambridge.

1956 Watson returns to the United States and becomes a biology professor at Harvard University.

1959 Arthur Kornberg and Severo Ochoa receive a

Nobel Prize in medicine for creating genetic material outside of a living cell.

1962 Francis Crick teaches at Harvard as a visiting professor in biophysics.

December 10—James Watson, Francis Crick, and Maurice Wilkins accept the Nobel Prize for physiology or medicine.

1968 *The Double Helix* by James Watson is published. Watson is named director of Cold Spring Harbor Laboratory.

1976 Crick moves to the United States to work at the Salk Institute for Biological Studies.

1979 Watson helps to establish the European Molecular Biology Organization.

1980s The British Broadcasting Company produces a film about Watson and Crick.

1988 Human Genome Initiative is formed with James Watson as associate director.

1993 Crick's book about consciousness, *The Astonishing Hypothesis*, is published.

Glossary

atheist A person who does not believe in the existence of God.

bacterial viruses Viruses that attack bacteria.

bacteriophages Bacterial viruses.

botany The study of plants.

cell The microscopic unit that is the building block of all living things.

chemical bonding The process by which atoms join together to form molecules of different substances.

chromosomes Long, coiled, threadlike matter found in all living cells and viruses that stores genetic information.

cloning The process by which a genetically identical organism is produced by replacing an unfertilized egg cell's nucleus with a nucleus of a specialized cell (i.e. stomach).

cytology The study of cells.

DNA (deoxyribonucleic acid) A nucleic acid found in all living cells. DNA carries hereditary information from parent to offspring.

enzymes A group of proteins that control the speed of chemical reactions in the body.

extinct No longer in existence.

gene One of the units found on a chromosome that determines the characteristics that an offspring inherits from its parent.

gene splicing The process of transferring a gene from one chromosome to another, usually in a different organism.

genetic engineer A scientist who studies and performs gene splicing.

genetics A branch of biology that examines heredity and the inherited differences and similarities found in living things.

globular proteins A group of proteins that do not have a regular geometric shape.

helix Any object having a spiral shape.

hemoglobin A substance in red blood cells that gives them their color and carries oxygen throughout the body.

heredity The process by which traits are transmitted from parent to offspring.

molecular biology A branch of biology that examines the physical and chemical make-up of living things.

molecule The smallest particle of a substance that retains all the properties of the substance.

mutations Changes that occur in the genes of a parent and that are inheritable.

neurons The basic units of the nervous system.

nucleic acids Organic compounds that are found in all living cells, that store the inherited traits of all living things. DNA and RNA are the two main kinds of nucleic acids.

nucleotides Any of many different compounds that are the basic structural units of nucleic acids.

nucleus A small round or oval body often found near the center of a plant or animal cell that contains most of the cell's hereditary material.

ornithology The study of birds.

protein synthesis The process by which different amino acids are made into proteins.

purines One group of nitrogen-containing bases (adenine and guanine) comprising nucleotides.

pyrimidines One group of nitrogen-containing bases (cytosine, thymine, and uracil) comprising nucleotides.

quantum mechanics A branch of physics that explains the physical forces holding an atom together.

retrovirus A virus that is made of RNA instead of DNA and that can duplicate itself by copying the DNA code in reverse.

RNA (ribonucleic acid) A nucleic acid found in all living cells.

species A group of organisms that shares many traits with one another and that can reproduce with one another.

subatomic particles Particles that are smaller than an atom and are the basic components of nature; electrons, protons, and neutrons are subatomic particles.

x-ray crystallography The process by which the structure of a crystallized substance is determined by aiming x-rays through its molecules.

x-ray diffraction The process by which x-rays are scattered by the atoms of a crystal.

Further Reading

Aaseng, Nathan. *Charles Darwin: Revolutionary Biologist.* Minneapolis, MN: Lerner, 1993.

Asimov, Isaac. *How Did We Find Out About DNA?* New York: Walker & Co., 1985.

Bornstein, Sandy. *What Makes You What You Are? A First Look at Genetics.* New York: Simon and Schuster, 1989.

Crick, Francis. *What Mad Pursuit?* New York: Basic Books, 1988.

——. *The Astonishing Hypothesis.* New York: Scribners, 1993.

Edelson, Edward. *Genetics and Heredity.* New York: Chelsea House, 1991.

Lampton, Christopher. *DNA Fingerprinting.* New York: Watts, 1991.

Newton, David. *James Watson and James Crick.* New York: Facts On File, 1992.

Serafini, Anthony. *Linus Pauling: A Man and His Science.* New York: Paragon House, 1989.

Sherrow, Victoria. *Jonas Salk.* New York: Facts On File, 1993.

Silverstein, Alvin, and Silverstein, Virginia B. *Genes, Medicine, and You.* Hillside, NJ: Enslow, 1989.

Thro, Ellen. *Genetic Engineering.* New York: Facts On File, 1993.

Watson, James Dewey and Tooze, John. *The DNA Story: A Documentary History of Gene Cloning.* San Francisco: W. H. Freeman, 1981.

Watson, James Dewey. *The Double Helix.* New York: Atheneum, 1968.

Young, John K. *Cells: Amazing Forms and Functions.* New York: Watts, 1990.

Index

Acknowledgements

The publisher would like to thank Jim Trifone for expertly reviewing the manuscript and Clare Bunce at Cold Spring Harbor Laboratory Archives for helping to locate photographic materials.

Photo Credits

LAKE COUNTY PUBLIC LIBRARY
INDIANA

X